Library of
Davidson College

The Making of Music

Ralph Vaughan Williams

The Making of Music

RALPH VAUGHAN WILLIAMS

GREENWOOD PRESS, PUBLISHERS
WESTPORT, CONNECTICUT

Library of Congress Cataloging in Publication Data

Vaughan Williams, Ralph, 1872-1958.
   The making of music.

   Reprint of the ed. published by Cornell University
Press, Ithaca, N.Y.
    1. Music--Addresses, essays, lectures. I. Title.
ML60.V287 1976   780   76-1009
ISBN 0-8371-8771-0

Copyright 1955 by Cornell University

Originally published in 1955 by Cornell University Press,
Ithaca, New York

Reprinted with the permission of Cornell University Press

Reprinted in 1976 by Greenwood Press,
a division of Williamhouse-Regency Inc.

Library of Congress Catalog Card Number 76-1009

ISBN 0-8371-8771-0

Printed in the United States of America

Preface

THIS volume contains the substance, though not necessarily the actual words, of a series of four lectures given at Cornell University in the autumn of 1954. I have made some omissions and some additions; the epilogue is adapted from a lecture given at Yale University on December 1, 1954.

Professor Donald Grout has read through my typescript and has given me much good advice, for which I am grateful.

R. VAUGHAN WILLIAMS

Contents

1. *Why do we make music?*   1
2. *What is music?*   3
   Melody – Rhythm – Harmony
3. *How do we make music?*   17
   Notation – Inspiration – Craft – Instruments
4. *When do we make music?*   35
   Ceremony – Dance – Words and music – Social background
5. *What are the social foundations of music?*   45
6. *The Folk-Song Movement*   49

   Epilogue: Making Your Own Music   53

The Making of Music

[1]

Why do we make music?

WHY do we make music? There can be no doubt that at certain emotional moments most people want to make particular kinds of noises. Indeed, we may say with Carlyle that if we search deep enough there is music everywhere. But why? Neither I, nor anyone else, has been able to solve that problem. But one thing we can be certain of: we do not compose, sing, or play music for any useful purpose. It is not so with the other arts: Milton had to use the medium of words whether he was writing *Paradise Lost* or making out his laundry list; Velasquez had to use paint both for his *Venus* and to cover up the dirty marks on his front door. But music is just music, and that is, to my mind, its great glory. How then do I justify music? There is no need to justify it, it is its own justification; that is all I know and all I need to know.

[2]

What is music?

BEFORE we go further we had better have a definition of what we mean by music, and I would define it thus: music is a reaching out to the ultimate realities by means of ordered sound. By "ordered sound" I mean sounds of a definite pitch in a definite rhythm and, perhaps we should add, with a definite harmony. But it may be asked what does music mean? A lot of nonsense is talked nowadays about the "meaning" of music. Music indeed has a meaning, though it is not one that can be expressed in words. Mendelssohn used to say that the meaning of music was too precise for words. The hearer may, of course, if he chooses, narrow the meaning of music to fit words or visual impressions, as for example in opera. But this particularisation limits the scope of music. The fire on Brünnhilde's rock may have suggested Wagner's music to him; but the music goes further and transports us from the particular to the universal. Liszt used to talk rather foolishly about it being nobler for a piece of music to be about Orpheus than to be a mere pattern in sound, not realising that it is these great patterns in sound, designed by Beethoven or Bach, which open the magic casements and enable us to understand what is beyond the appearances of life.

There are two theories of how these ordered sounds arose. Some people think that they grew out of excited speech, some that they developed from blowing through a pipe pierced at definite intervals with holes.

I do not want to set up my opinion against that of those learned musicologists who hold the pipe theory. But an ounce of experience is worth a pound of speculation, and I want to describe a personal experience, when I actually heard excited speech grow into melody. I once heard a sermon at an open-air service in the Isle of Skye. As the preacher spoke in Gaelic, which I do not understand, I was able to devote my attention to the actual tones of his voice. The fact that he was out of doors forced him to speak loud, and that, coupled with the emotional excitement which inspired his words, caused him gradually to leave off speaking and actually, unconsciously of course, to sing. At first he was content with a monotone, but as his excitement grew, he gradually evolved the following melodic formulae:

Now these melodic formulae are common to the opening of many Scottish and British folk songs; here are two examples:

"Bushes and Briars"

"Searching for Lambs"[1]

This experience has convinced me that these melodic formulae come spontaneously to the minds of primitive singers. We can hardly believe that our preacher obtained his notes by blowing through a mathematically measured pipe. I have lately read a book by the Reverend George Chambers in which he describes how in primitive religious services the logical meaning of the words spoken proved inadequate and was supplemented by song, including cantilenas on pure vowel sounds, which were called "jubilations"; these evidently had a mystical meaning to their singers that words could not give them.

[1] From *English Folk Songs*, collected and arranged by Cecil J. Sharp, selected ed. (London: Novello and Co., n.d.), I, 74. By permission.

Indeed, as I have already said, the meaning of music is beyond words.

We now come to the question of rhythm. What is rhythm? I have tried various sources for a satisfactory definition and have, so far, failed. Frank Howes, the musical critic of the London *Times*, calls it "an innate faculty for the apprehension of time." Here is Professor Carl Seashore's definition: "An instinctive disposition to group recurrent sense impressions vividly and with precision, mainly by time or intensity, or both, in such a way as to derive pleasure and efficiency through the grouping." I cannot see that either of these is very helpful. Other writers talk magniloquently about the importance of rhythm, not only in art, but in life, without troubling to explain what they mean when they talk about the rhythm of life. (Incidentally, I much dislike the modern practice of using the technical terms of one art to illustrate another, as when one speaks of the tempo of an essay, or the orchestration of a picture, or the rhythm of a building.) Perhaps the word is indefinable. A French musician is reported to have said to a lady who asked him what rhythm was, "Madame, if you have already rhythm in your nature, there is no need for me to explain it to you; if you have not, you would not understand my explanation." Or there is Lord Haldane's famous epigram: "I cannot define an elephant, but I recognise one when I see it." In the same way, without being able to explain it, those who are naturally musical can appreciate rhythm, or the want of it, in a piece of music.

Here are one or two examples of the way in which a

very slight alteration in rhythm can entirely change the nature of a melody. Compare the opening of Brahms's B-flat Pianoforte Concerto with the "Inter oves" from Verdi's *Requiem*. Both extracts are in the same key, their notes are identical—except for one slight rhythmical change. But how extraordinarily different they sound.

Pianoforte Concerto in B-flat—Brahms

"Inter oves" from the *Requiem*—Verdi

Here is another, stronger example. The well-known English dance tune, "Sellenger's Round," apparently crossed over to Germany, and by the ironing out of the rhythm became converted from a lively dance measure to a solemn hymn tune.

"Sellenger's Round"

etc.

"Valet will ich"—J. S. Bach, after Teschner

etc.

7

And as a climax I will quote from Edmund Gurney's *The Power of Sound,* in which by rhythmical distortion he converts the magnificent chorale melody, "Ein' feste Burg," into a vulgar jig tune.

"Ein' feste Burg"—J. S. Bach, after Luther

The same as distorted by Gurney

In this connection it must be confessed that the tune as Martin Luther is supposed to have played it on his flute to his family seems rather a poor affair; it was left to Bach to develop it into magnificence in his Cantata No. 80.

The Greek word *rhythmos* means "flow"; so flow may be taken to be an essential part of rhythm. An orderly succession of sounds at regular intervals is also a part of rhythm, but it is not, as many people imagine, the whole of rhythm. The ticking of a clock, for example, is not rhythmical, because it has no periodic accents. Some years ago an American, Dr. Thaddeus Lincoln Bolton, made the following experiment: A machine like a clock, with absolutely regular ticks but without any accent, was set going, and several people were asked to give their impression of what they heard. Almost all said that after a certain number of ticks, usually three or four, the next appeared louder. This was a purely mental illusion and was due to the desire for rhythmical quality implicit in their nature. This gives us another principle of rhythm, that of strong and weak accent, which the monks of Solesmes in their treatise on plainsong describe as *élan et repos*. This principle has been called by other writers "exertion and rest," or "impulse and relax." The Greeks, in their poetry, used the words *arsis* and *thesis*, "rising and falling," to describe the rhythmical qualities of poetic metres. Incidentally, both these words are derived from dancing.

I wish now to digress a moment to say something about rhythm in poetry. Rhythm is as essential to poetry as it is to music, and as we cannot have rhythm without time in music, so we cannot have poetical rhythm without metre. But the rhythm of poetry is something more than this. Is not the caesura a momentary breaking of the metre for the sake of the larger aspect of rhythm? In poetry there are always two kinds of accent, that supplied by the sense of the passage and that supplied by the nature of the metre. Often these coincide, but sometimes they are at variance, as when the meaning of a passage carries on over the end of a line. There is the well-known story of the little girl who complained to her mother that she did not want her grave to be as little as her bed. She had been singing the words,

> Teach me to live that I may dread
> The grave, as little as my bed.

When she sang it with the tune, it became,

> Teach me to live that I may dread,
> The grave as little as my bed.

Another humourous example of this cross accent is the clown's prologue in *A Midsummer Night's Dream*.

I should like to add one personal experience. I was setting to music one of Gilbert Murray's translations of Euripides, and I came upon these lines:

> Only on them that spurn
> Joy, may his anger burn.[2]

I pointed out to Professor Murray that if I set the words strictly according to their meaning, it would convert the verse into prose:

> Only on them that spurn joy, may his anger burn.

If I set it strictly according to the metre, it would make nonsense of the words:

> Only on them that spurn,
> Joy may his anger burn.

He solved my difficulties by declaiming the lines to me in a manner which I can describe only by musical notation:

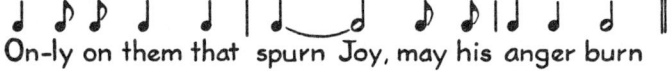

[2] From *The Bacchae*, ll. 425–426, in *The Complete Greek Drama*, ed. by Whitney J. Oates and Eugene O'Neill, Jr. (New York: Random House, 1938), II, 241. By permission of George Allen & Unwin.

From the question of rhythm we pass naturally to the question of form, which is, after all, nothing more than rhythm on a large scale. We often hear people say, "I know nothing about musical form, but I like a good tune when I hear it." They do not realise that to appreciate the simplest tune requires a knowledge of form. The physical ear can hear only one sound, or a vertical group of sounds, at a time; the rest is a question of memory, co-ordination, and anticipation. When the first note passes on to the second, the hearer must not only keep the first note in memory, but co-ordinate it with the second, and so on to the third; and occasionally he has to anticipate what is to come. When community singers are learning a new tune, they often get the tune wrong because they anticipate a different note from what actually comes. If we did not have these powers, the simplest tune would be meaningless. To appreciate the "Hammerklavier" Sonata or the Ninth Symphony requires exactly the same qualities as the appreciation of the simplest tune—such as "The Bluebell of Scotland," which any child can learn—only to a greater degree. Musical form is not a series of mysteries or trade secrets but is simply the development of a power natural to the human ear and the human mind. To understand a big symphonic work there is no need to look up textbooks or memorise regulations; one need only develop the qualities of attention, memory, and co-ordination to the utmost. One thing, however, is needful: the whole passage, whether it be a folk tune or a symphony, must grow, organically, from its roots.

This leads us on to the question of form and content. These two words are often taken to mean separate and opposite parts of an artistic structure. We talk about the form of a sonata being good and its content poor; but is not the content poor because the form is bad? And so we go on, ad infinitum. It is the content which settles the form of any organic structure.

What, after all, is good content? Is it not a matter of suitability to its purpose? The opening theme of the "Eroica" Symphony is just an arpeggio, and not original at that, but what a wonderful foundation for a great movement! The famous drum passage at the end of the Scherzo of Beethoven's C-minor Symphony would not, without its context, be evidence of the mind of a great composer; but coming where it does, as a sort of resurrection from the abyss, at the end of the Scherzo, and then building up on those reiterated drum taps into the glorious outburst of the finale, does it not reveal the master mind at work? The theme connected with the Rheingold in Wagner's *Ring* is a little flourish such as any boy bugler might have invented. But coming where it does, its dramatic effect is overwhelming. In all these cases there is organic connection between the whole and the parts. This organic connection can also exist between symphonic themes which have little physical resemblance. The second subject of the finale of Mozart's G-minor Symphony runs as follows:

When it reappears in the recapitulation, it is hardly recognisable, mechanically speaking, as the same theme. But its inevitable rightness in its place and its organic connection with the original idea make it a true development.

Now comes the question of harmony. It is doubtful whether this should count as a fundamental element of music, because, so far as we can make out, primitive music had no harmony but was purely melodic. This is true, so far as we can tell, of the early Greek music. The word *harmonia* does not mean harmony in our sense of the word, but the relation to each other of the notes in the Greek modes. The same is true of the plainsong of the early Christian church, and folk song, at all events in western Europe, was sung without harmonic accompaniment. However, it seems almost impossible that harmony should not have occurred to primitive singers and players, if only by accident. A cithara player must occasionally have twanged two strings at the same time; or if two pipe players happened to be playing at the same time within hearing distance of each other, this must have resulted in harmony, or even counterpoint. Why did not the performers carry on with the good work? The only explanation can be that when they heard the result they disliked it. There is no physical reason why an eighteenth-century composer should not have written the whole of Stravinsky and Schönberg, provided he had the pen and paper. We know as a fact that Stanley, an eighteenth-century English composer, experimented with the whole-tone scale about a hundred years before Debussy. Here are two examples, one from Mozart's quartet in C major and one from Haydn's Prelude to *The Creation*, which anticipate Wagner's *Tristan*.

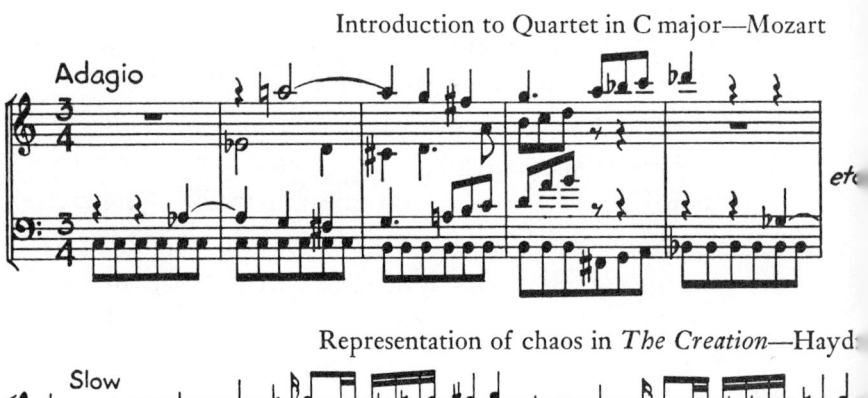

These harmonies were, for these two composers, obviously an experiment; they had no emotional significance for them. For Wagner, an almost identical passage symbolised the height of amorous passion. To Haydn and Mozart they had no such suggestion. When Mozart wanted to be erotic he wrote "Là ci darem."

Now let us look at the obverse of the medal. Debussy's strange atmospheric effects still thrill us, though they are by now the common property of every conservatory student. And when these same students write out bits of Debussy, under the impression that they are composing, their efforts fall dead even before the ink is dry. The moral of all this seems to be that any musical phrase, to be a complete artistic whole, must be the result of a personal emotion.

These, then, are the three elements which go to make up music—melody, rhythm, and harmony.

[3]

How do we make music?

AMONG the foundations of our art we can count the means by which the singer or player communicates his ideas to others—what we call musical notation. But first I want to try to dispose of a very prevalent fallacy. My old teacher, Max Bruch, used to say to me, "You must not write eye music, you must write ear music." He, at all events, had got hold of the truth. But many musical writers who ought to know better think that music is not what we hear with our ears but what we see on the printed or written page; and some of them say with pride that they never want to hear music, it is enough for them to see the score. I suppose I must take them at their word that they can tell exactly what the music will sound like by reading it.

Now music differs from the sister art of poetry in that the emotion of poetry grows out of the meaning of words and can be achieved as well by reading as by hearing. If you listen to a poem recited in a language you do not understand, you get very little of the emotion that the poem is intended to express. Sometimes, indeed, you get something quite different, as in the ludicrous case of the audience at Covent Garden who, when the prisoners in *Fidelio* were whispering "leise, leise," tittered with amusement because they were reminded of a popular song of the day about a young lady called 'Liza.

Many people imagine that a printed page of music is the equivalent of a painted picture; but the painter has a dual nature, he is both composer and performer. A picture is the finished article; but this is not so with a page of music, which is, at the best, a rough description of what the composer hopes will happen if the sounds he has indicated by certain symbols are produced in actuality. Until this takes place the music does not exist. A page of music should be compared, not to a picture, but to a map, which indicates by certain conventional signs where north and south are, the direction of a road, what sort of road it is, how high the hills are, whether they are steep or gradual, where there are buildings, and so on. The expert map reader, like the expert score reader, may be able to tell fairly exactly what sort of country he may expect to find, but he cannot possibly experience the beauty of the trees, the intense emotion of a wonderful landscape, the exhilaration of rushing down hill on a bicycle, or the delightful relaxation when he reaches the comfortable inn, indicated, in England at all events, by the magic letters "P.H." So it is with the score reader. Haydn would never have declared that his great shout, "Let there be light!" came straight from heaven if he had been content to read the music and not hear it. Nor would Ulysses have been obliged to be tied to the mast if the Sirens, instead of singing to him, had given him a presentation copy of the full score.

In primitive times a written score was unnecessary because the composer and the performer were the same individual, who wanted to touch the heart of those, only, who were within hearing distance. But supposing the musician's fame grew and people far off wanted to hear his music, what was to be done then? He must invent and write out a series of symbols which will say in effect, "If you sing, blow, scratch, or hit exactly according to the directions here given, you will make the same sound as I have been imagining." Or, to put it in another way, the composer has a vision and he wants others, out of earshot, to share that vision; so he crystallises that vision into definite musical sounds. Then he devises a series of black dots, circles, and so on which will explain what sounds must be made in order to realise his vision. This is what is called musical notation. It is notoriously inadequate, so that those who translate these symbols into music are bound by their personal equation and each performs slightly differently. Thus come about what we call the different renderings by great performers or conductors of the same music. Those who are going to translate these black dots into sound must first find out how to use them adequately. Also, they must learn to realise, when the sounds are made, the connection between the various notes which they produce and the ultimate meaning of it all. Then, and then only, can they realise in sound the vision that has passed through all these stages and back again to arrive once more at the magic casements and the fairyland which lies beyond them.

What are the sources of a composer's inspiration? Now inspiration and originality do not necessarily mean something no one has ever heard before. To my mind the most original of present-day composers is Jean Sibelius. All he says in his great moments seems to me absolutely new; but his actual method of diction is purely traditional. As Hans Sachs said of Walther, "It was so old, it sounded so new."

We often find that music which at its first appearance seemed *outré*, to the dismay of the audience and the delight of the composer, becomes quite outmoded after a few years and gives way to a new method of shocking the bourgeois. In Leipzig, in the eighteenth century, Bach was already considered an old fogey, and all the bright young things swore by Telemann. Bach, after a period of eclipse, has come back into his own, while Telemann only bores us.

When Liszt produced his well-known pianoforte concerto, it was hailed by one school of German thought as something new and incomprehensible to the public, while Brahms was condemned as being *routinier* and academic. Now Brahms sounds as fresh as ever, while, to one hearer at least, the music of Liszt seems intolerably old-fashioned.

Therefore I beg all young composers not to try to be original, within the narrow sense of the word. Originality will come of itself if it is in one's nature. This does not mean that the composer must be careless and thoughtless. It is hard, indeed, to find a true expression of one's vision. But the artist must not rest until he has discovered the *mot juste.* If another composer has said the same thing before, so much the worse for the other composer. The originality, or perhaps I should say the personality, of music depends very little on the actual outline of the notes. It derives from something more subtle, which perhaps we cannot define but can recognise at once. Schumann used to say that Beethoven's chromatic scales sounded different from other people's. Here are three fugue subjects, each distinct and individual, but built up on the same phrase:

"And with His stripes"—Handel

Forty-eight Preludes and Fugues, No. 20, from Book II (transposed)—Bach

Kyrie from the *Requiem* (transposed)—Mozart

One of the most important elements of our art is the craft which must inevitably accompany it—the craft of the composer, the performer, and the instrument maker. These three are inseparably connected. The player must have something to play; the composer is impotent unless there is someone to realise his ideas; and both of them are lost, except of course in the case of vocal music, unless there is someone who can devise and construct a machine to carry out the composer's ideas through the skill of the performer.

In primitive times these three persons were probably merged in one: a man thought of a tune; next he had to cut a reed and pierce it with holes so as to make the noises he needed; then he had to acquire enough skill to make these noises. But perhaps things did not always happen in that order. Perhaps he heard a song tune and, having a sore throat, wanted to realise it in some other way. Or perhaps, like the lady in "The Lost Chord," his "fingers wandered idly Over the noisy keys" until he found something that he liked. Or perhaps he made the pipe first and in trying it out hit upon a good tune.

These methods still exist in modern times. We are told in textbooks that a composer must write down his ideas without going near an instrument. Indeed "composing at the pianoforte" was described by R. O. Morris as "not quite playing the game." Nevertheless it is a practice that I hope all young composers will indulge in freely, when they are in the mood and the teacher is out of earshot. Inspiration does not necessarily come from the brain. Unfortunately, one cannot play the pianoforte with one's solar plexus, but I see no reason why ideas should not ooze out of the finger tips. Maurice Ravel used to blame me for trying to compose without using a pianoforte, saying, "How then can you invent new harmonies?" I do not suggest to composers that they should invent, like the young genius in the films, with one hand holding a pen and the other improvising at the pianoforte, but I can see no moral harm, and great artistic advantage, in making certain of our ideas by trying them over and exploring their possibilities at the pianoforte.

Where does craft end and art begin? When I first heard the Prelude to *Lohengrin*, I wondered how Wagner had devised all those wonderful high string effects. But when I saw the full score I realised that I, or any other composer, would have done the same *if only we had thought of the music.* I was like the schoolboy who said, "I could easily have written all that Shakespeare stuff myself if I'd only thought of it."

Craft by itself can do nothing, I admit, and in some ways is a dangerous thing. When a composer of great skill finds his invention at a low ebb, he can still write music which almost deceives the elect, and he himself sometimes cannot tell whether he is inspired or whether he is doing mere routine work. Nevertheless, the most inspired composer is impotent unless his craft keeps pace with his art.

It is now fashionable to teach children painting without any technical training. They are given a paintbox and a brush and told to "express themselves." I have seen the results. The children could not draw a straight line and had no idea of anatomy or perspective. When I pointed this out to the drawing mistress, she rebuked me and told me that the "feeling" was wonderful. Fortunately, in music we still believe,to a certain extent, in technique. But, in England at all events, we are no longer allowed to speak of harmony and counterpoint but must call our theoretic studies "paper work." I am glad to say that I was brought up in the traditional manner. I worked right through MacFarren's *Harmony* and the Cherubinic system of counterpoint and have never regretted it. At a recent meeting of modern composers the only thing they all agreed on was that the only sure foundation for musical composition was strict counterpoint.

We now come to a very important factor in our art, the means by which we make the necessary noises. The chief of these is the human voice, which has been called the perfect instrument—perfect in the sense that there is a minimum of mechanism between the initial impulse and the result. The voice in this respect is unlike the oboe or horn, in which the connection is not so direct between the performer's will and the sound he makes.

The scope of the human voice is, of course, limited. The range of the four main voices, bass, tenor, contralto, and soprano, is not more than four octaves, from C below the bass clef to c''' above the treble clef, except in the case of Russian basses and freak sopranos. On the other hand, the art of singing is nearly universal; most people can sing a bit. Moreover, the technique and the nature of the human voice is very much what it was two thousand years ago. This is why choral music has remained in the straight road much more than has instrumental writing. In *a cappella* singing there are no instrument makers to lure the composer aside with exciting new devices. When Stravinsky writes his *Symphony of Psalms*, one can feel that he is dealing with something fundamental, almost primitive. In the choral music of Copland the tradition of the white spiritual unconsciously affects his music. Music for voices deals with something essential, not with the tricks of presentation.

Whether the instrument or voice came first, there can be very little doubt that the pipe and harp appear very soon in primitive music, and the question arises, Was it the inventions of instrument makers which enticed composers into new styles of music or was it the imperious demands of the composers for fresh means of expression which led the instrument makers to see what they could do to help? We can imagine that Strephon made a pipe for Amaryllis to play the little tunes that she had invented; did Amaryllis say that her new tune demanded an extra hole in the pipe, or did Strephon tell Amaryllis that he had pierced a new hole and expected her, forthwith, to make use of it?

Up to the sixteenth century music was almost entirely vocal, unable to move very fast, but capable of holding a sound for a long time. Then came the development of the lute and virginals, unable to sustain sounds like the voice but able to play very quickly. So composers of virginal music invented a new means of covering the ground by the use of elaborate scales and arpeggios, as we find in the final cadences of almost all virginal music. These limitations and new capabilities led the way from the pure choral counterpoint of Palestrina to the instrumental polyphony of Bach. For the harpsichord, though it could not hold long notes, could play the quick passages and could achieve phrases and intervals which would be unsingable by unaccompanied voices.

Bach's style, even in his vocal works, has an instrumental foundation. I have it on the authority of Tovey that Bach never wrote for unaccompanied chorus. Even in his motets and chorales the voices were doubled by instruments, which enabled them to achieve passages that they could not have sung unaccompanied, with the result that a choral technique developed. Nowadays we often sing these compositions *a cappella*, and to my mind they sound very beautiful that way. We are told that we are wrong to perform them thus because that was not what Bach intended. Are we so sure that he did not so intend them, but was prevented by the inadequacy of the means at his disposal?

Sir George Dyson once said to me that in his opinion Bach never heard a decent performance of one of his cantatas or motets. We know that he complained bitterly of the inferiority of his players and singers. Are we not then justified in modifying his instrumentation where it is obvious that he was buying a pig in a poke?

There is good evidence that Bach was prepared to cut his suit according to his cloth, an instance being the beautiful passage for the lute from the *St. John Passion*, to which Bach appended a note that if necessary it could be played on the organ! In Bach's time the pianoforte had only just been invented, and he is reported to have commented unfavourably on the imperfect examples which were shown him by Frederick the Great. Tovey was of the opinion that if Bach had known a modern grand pianoforte he would have preferred its tone to the nasty jangle of the harpsichord to which he was condemned for filling in his continuo.

This question of the continuo, or figured bass, requires a little more consideration. If we look at a full score of an aria from a Bach Passion or the B-minor Mass, we find something very different from what appears in the vocal score editions. In the full score we see the voice part and, usually, only the bass, with perhaps a line for an obbligato instrument. The bass sometimes has figures under it to indicate what the inner parts are to be. The director, or his substitute, sat at the harpsichord or organ improvising these inner parts and generally keeping the whole performance together.

What initiated this continuo system? The music of the great choral period, the sixteenth century, made use of no such device. The figured bass arose from weakness rather than from strength. About the year 1600 some Italian amateurs devised the beginnings of opera. They had very little technical knowledge of music and therefore left the filling in of the harmony, we may suppose, to some professional expert, indicating to him only the bass and the voice parts. This was all very well for a recitative, accompanied by a few chords, but to hear a large choral work thickened out by the continual presence of the harpsichord or organ must have become intolerably monotonous. But it obtained all through the eighteenth century until the advent of the conductor and the increased efficiency of the performers made it unnecessary. But even now, in solo songs of the Bach period, we usually have to use some instrument to fill up the inner parts. A good grand pianoforte does this much less obtrusively and more artistically than the harpsichord. But I am sorry to say that in obedience to the new Bach-as-he-wrote-it fashion this instrument is again raising its unpleasant head.

The clarinet is a good example of the way in which an instrument will stimulate a composer. It was not an inevitable part of the orchestra in the time of Bach and Handel; it belonged chiefly to the open-air wind band and was, I imagine, a coarse and rather loud instrument, as its name, "little trumpet," suggests. But in the early eighteenth century the conductor of the well-known Mannheim orchestra added what must have been an improved version of the clarinet to his band. It was here that Mozart heard this beautiful instrument, for which he later wrote a concerto. He also added a clarinet part to the score of his G-minor Symphony. Haydn followed suit, first using the instrument rather tentatively to fill up the tuttis; but when he wrote the Prelude to *The Creation*, he had fully realised its possibilities. Here then is a case of the instrument maker prompting the composer.

It was just the opposite with Wagner and his tubas: he wanted four of these instruments to suggest Valhalla, in the *Ring*—higher in pitch and rather thinner in tone than the ordinary bass tuba. So he set to work with an instrument maker and together they devised the so-called Wagner tubas.

I fear that it is the mid-nineteenth-century composers who are to blame for the deterioration of the modern horn and trumpet. They were continually demanding from the trumpet higher and higher notes and from the horn more and more agility, with the result that the noble old trumpet in F had to be given up in favour of a tinny little instrument in a higher key and the true French horn, the soul of orchestral poetry, disappeared in favour of an instrument which looks, indeed, like a horn but sounds more like a mixture of a saxophone and a euphonium. All of Richard Strauss's tricks can be played easily on this instrument, and it is said to be quite safe and never to bubble, but its poetry is gone. A few years ago I heard the opening of Schubert's C-major Symphony played on a real horn, and all the world beyond the world seemed open to me. Later on I heard it played on a modern instrument; the notes were as certain as if they were being played on an organ, but the magic was no longer there.

Hubert Parry used to say that the beauty of the French horn was partly due to its human fallibility. Is not this true, to a certain extent, of all instrumental playing? Does not the thrill of sixteen violins playing together come from the fact that they are not scientifically in tune with each other? Would not the wonderful surge of the opening of Schubert's "Unfinished" Symphony be lost if the violoncellos and basses moved from note to note with mathematical exactness at the same moment? An orchestra must not become a perfect machine.

Now comes the question of making the instrument first and finding the music for it afterwards. Berlioz is the great sinner in this respect. He did not, of course, make instruments himself, but he thought out such devices as the four brass bands in the *Messe des morts*, and in the excitement of the invention of the means forgot about the end. When it came to the point, he could think of nothing better for his four brass bands to play than a banal march tune. This was indeed putting the cart before the horse. And so the old problem of form and content crops up again; the idea and its presentation should be simultaneous and indivisible.

I have purposely reserved for special discussion the most important instrument in our modern musical armoury. The pianoforte is a comparatively new invention. It was a long time before it superseded the clavichord as a household instrument and the harpsichord for public use. The famous organ builder, Gottfried Silbermann, made some experimental pianofortes for Frederick the Great; Bach tried them and, it is reported, did not care for them. Probably these early examples were very imperfect. The early manufacturers made the mistake of trying to make the pianoforte sound like a harpsichord. Even Beethoven's pianoforte was a very different affair from our modern grand.

Gradually the new instrument acquired its own character and atmosphere. The tone of the harpsichord was constant: only by the manipulation of stops and manuals could the player vary from loud to soft, while crescendo and diminuendo were impossible. A good player on a modern pianoforte can pass at will, gradually or quickly, from an almost inaudible softness to a thundering loudness, and this almost entirely by finger pressure, which has no more effect on the harpsichord than it does on the organ. The pianist can pick out a phrase for special prominence in the middle of a contrapuntal web in a manner that was impossible to his predecessor; by the use of the loud pedal he can prolong the sound of a note and thus evoke the idea of a violin or vocal cantabile. A clever pianist can suggest the orchestra, the organ, or even the choir, by his playing and can often get much nearer to the composer's idea than a second-rate orchestra.

Not only can a pianoforte look forward, it can also look back. Music written for the earlier instruments can also be played with good effect on the pianoforte. It may not be exactly what the composer intended, but composers are bound by their means, and I have little doubt that Bach would have thought that his music sounded better on our modern instruments than on those which he had at his disposal. I have heard many of the Forty-Eight Preludes and Fugues played alternately on the pianoforte and harpsichord, and I have no doubt which I prefer. For one thing, on the harpsichord the music sounded like "period music." To deprive a composition of its period might be fatal to something which is only of its period. Though Bach belongs superficially to the eighteenth century, spiritually he belongs equally to the twentieth. Therefore we can interpret him by our own minds and means and find that he lives for us, more than for the burghers of Leipzig; for them Bach was indeed the music of the future.

There is a modern fashion, originating, I believe, in Germany, of playing Bach's music "as he wrote it," which, as I suppose, means that we must, if possible, use the exact instruments which Bach used, presumably at the same pitch, and play them exactly as the eighteenth-century musicians played them—violins with flat bridges and bows held taut by the thumb. We should, of course, substitute the harpsichord for the pianoforte and make use of that atrocious bubble-and-squeak monstrosity, the so-called baroque organ. Our oboes would have to bray like bagpipes and our horns bellow like bulls. Well, we cannot do this even if we wanted to, and if we could, I cannot imagine anyone wanting to substitute the coarse tone and asthmatic phrasing of Bach's oboe for the exquisite cantabile of one of our fine symphonic players in the great watching song from the *Matthew Passion*.

The pianoforte at its best is now the universal provider, and at its worst, the maid of all work in our musical commonwealth. At one moment the pianoforte can be used to realise the most ethereal fancies of Chopin or Debussy and at another, to thump out a comic song in a tavern. The pianoforte is equally at home in the palace or the cottage and has a colossal specialised literature of every degree of goodness or badness. Thus the pianoforte has completed the democratisation of our art. The performer's intonation on a pianoforte does not depend on his own musical nature but on the state of his instrument. That is why for every one player on the flute or violin there are probably a hundred who can tap out a tune on the pianoforte. Here, then, is mass-made music for the masses; we must be careful that quantity does not oust quality.

May I put in a word for the pianoforte duet? When I was young and orchestral concerts were few, when full scores were beyond our means and the radio and phonograph were not yet invented, our chief means for studying orchestral music was the pianoforte duet. With all our modern aids to listening, we are too apt to hear music in a daydream, without giving it our real attention. But the pianoforte duet gave us an intimate knowledge of the great classics which we are all too likely to miss if we turn on the radio and the phonograph.

[4]

When do we make music?

MUSIC has always been part of ceremony, especially religious ceremony. From primitive times both song and dance have made part of religious ritual, which calls forth the desire for music, and especially song, to enhance the excitement and spiritual exaltation of the worshippers. The most important of these ceremonies for the last two thousand years have been those of the Roman church. In early days the priests had to wean their followers from the pagan festivals which they loved; so they built Christian churches on the sites of pagan temples and converted the gods of the Greek and Roman pantheons into companies of saints. Also, it is almost certain, they adapted the songs the people were already singing for use in their own services.

Father Chambers, well supported by quotations from the early fathers, argues that the melismata which are so characteristic of the Roman rite are adapted from the jubilations of primitive folk song. These were sung without words, which the people found to be inadequate, and they discovered a mystical meaning in these wordless cantilenas. When the church took over the jubilations, they found them difficult to memorise and they added to them words such as "alleluia" and "amen" and later whole poems as a sort of *aide-mémoire*. In the same way a folk singer will add words without meaning, such as "hey derry down," to help him remember the melody of a refrain. Not only did the church use these melismata for its own purposes, but it adapted whole ballads to ecclesiastical use, substituting pious words for the unseemly cries of the tavern love song. Father Chambers quotes a story of Brother Henry of Pisa, who, on hearing a servant girl sing a love song as she passed through the cathedral, was at once struck by the idea that the same tune could be set to religious words as a good means of converting the ungodly.

The same kind of thing has happened in modern times; in my own lifetime I have known the Salvation Army choirs to sing

> Ta-ra-ra-boom-de-ay
> We've saved a soul today.

John Wesley is reported to have said that he did not see why the Devil should have all the pretty tunes. True to his principles he set that superb hymn, "Lo he comes with clouds descending," to a popular tune known as

"Miss Catley's Hornpipe," which begins, "Where's the mortal can resist me?" I need hardly add that the original tune is nearly unrecognisable in its present stately form.

"Miss Catley's Hornpipe"
(Fast)

In the fifteenth century church composers began to use secular tunes as *canti fermi* on which to build their contrapuntal masses and motets. Almost every composer, including Palestrina, wrote a mass founded on the folk tune "L'homme armé." One English composer, Taverner, used a ballad tune, "Westron Wynd," as a *canto fermo* for a mass:

> O western wind when wilt thou blow
> That the small rain down may rain?
> Christ, that my love were in my arms
> And I in my bed again.

The congregations in the churches sometimes used to recognise these tunes, hidden though they were in the contrapuntal web (I fear that modern congregations might not be so clever), and having got hold of the tune they sang it, not to the words of the Mass, but to the original words of the folk song, which were, as we have seen, delightful in themselves but unsuitable for church use.

This state of affairs caused a scandal and led to a reform; Palestrina was called in to help and wrote the famous *Mass of Pope Marcellus*. But as we have seen, he still had a sneaking feeling for the old tunes, and sometimes he introduced a "tuney bit" into his music, such as the *Noe* from his "Hodie Christus natus est." The word *Noe* is not in the office and was probably an importation from a popular song. Perhaps Palestrina used the very tune to which the words were usually sung.

Noe from "Hodie Christus natus est"—Palestrina

There is also the well-known "Gloria" from his Magnificat in the Third Mode, which sounds much like a popular tune and is sung, in a slightly modified form, as a hymn tune to this day.

The same sort of thing was going on in France; in his book on French folk song Tiersot tells a wonderful tale of how, when Charlemagne brought his French church singers to Rome, the Romans complained of the rough, country character of their singing. What can this mean but that they were singing adapted popular songs? Now one of the psalm tunes which the French singers almost certainly brought with them is that known as the "Pilgrim's Tune," or "Tonus peregrinus." Another tune which they almost certainly sang was the famous Easter hymn, "O filii et filiae." Tiersot gives two French folk songs, "Rossignolet du bois" and "Voici venir le joli mois";[3] the resemblance between these songs and the two hymns can scarcely be accidental. What can be more likely than that the ecclesiastical musicians should have adapted such songs for their own hymns?

The Lutheran Reformation produced its own corpus of tunes. Some of these were specially composed, even by Luther himself; some were taken over from the Roman rite; and some were adaptations of popular songs, of which not only the tunes but the words were adapted for church use. The latter were called "spiritual parodies" of the originals. The best known of these is the famous tune "Innsbruck," which started life as "Innsbruck, ich muss dich lassen" but which became in the parody, "O Welt, ich muss dich lassen." The original was probably a nostalgic song by a wandering apprentice, leaving his native town; one can see how easily this could be changed to a spiritual meditation. There is a beautiful setting of the original tune by Heinrich Isaac. Then it found its way into church, where congrega-

---

[3] Julien Tiersot, *Histoire de la chanson populaire en France* (Paris: Plon, Nourrit et Cie., 1889), pp. 73, 361.

tional singing caused it to put on a strait waistcoat; it finally achieved immortality in Bach's *St. Matthew Passion*.

Another good example is a love song, "Flora, meine Freude." Here is one of the earliest versions of the tune, as given in Johannes Zahn's great collection, *Die Melodien der deutschen evangelischen Kirchenlieder*:

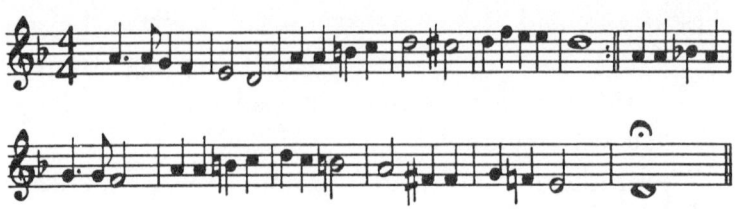

This song became, at the hands of the parodists, "Jesu, meine Freude." One version of the tune and the revised words became the basis of Bach's great motet of the same name.

The connection between music and dance is obvious: dance music is a specialised form of the art because the nature of the dance demands strong accents, a square pattern, and short phrases. Dance music is really applied art. I do not mean by this that dance is the justification of music; rather, music is the justification of the dance. Who would dream of dancing without music? Would not the dance alone become a series of meaningless antics? On the other hand, dance music is often played without the dance; the waltzes of Johann Strauss can arouse enthusiasm in the concert room until it is difficult to keep one's feet still. So we come to the old conclusion that beauty derives from suitability but often outlives its original purpose.

Miss Maud Karpeles, the well-known authority on folk song and former assistant of Cecil Sharp, writes as follows:

> The folk themselves are very conscious of the intimate connection between music and the dance. Mr. Sharp often had the experience that a dancer would sing him the tune and then be quite surprised if having learned the tune he could not tell how the dance went. One old dancer said to him, "We used to learn the song and then there was no trouble for the steps are just as the words be." From that one would imagine that the words were some kind of description of the dance, but usually they were just nonsense rhymes. For instance, the words of Greensleeves, the tune used for the Bacca Pipes Jig, are
>
> > Some say the devil's dead   (three times)
> > And buried in Cold Harbour
> >
> > Some say he's rose again   (three times)
> > And married to a barber.
>
> It is certainly a little difficult to see the connection between these words and the steps of the Jig, but the explanation is that the dancer felt that the words enforced the rhythm of the music and helped him to get hold of the tune and sing it himself. And once having got the tune inside him, so to speak, all was plain sailing.[4]

This brings us logically to our next consideration, that of words and music.

[4] From a letter to the author. By permission.

How far can we count language as one of the sources of music? Primitive singers, as we know, used music only as a means of memorising words or dances, but we have seen that, in the jubilus, music often gets beyond words, which then become mere vehicles for punctuating the vowel sounds. The word "Nowell," for example, which so often comes in the refrains of carols, probably means "good news," *nouvelles,* but from the singer's point of view, when coupled with the music, it transcends meaning and thus enters a mystical world.

Words when sung are sometimes only the framework for sound. Wagner used to read the libretti of his operas to his friends; I am glad I was not there. One could not fill the Metropolitan or Covent Garden with a spoken recital of the *Ring.* But one can excite an audience to enthusiasm in the concert room with the *Meistersinger* overture, or with the "Liebestod," though one may not be able to hear, or understand, any of the words sung by Isolde. This may indeed be an advantage, because her words, by themselves, are a very poor exposition of the situation. It is the music that reaches the sublimity of passion. Of course words are necessary in opera; the singers are there singing, and it would never do for them to declaim "la, la, la," all the time. However, in his lyrical moments Wagner was very clever in using words such as *Liebe, Nacht, ewig,* or even the names of the two protagonists, all of which have a strong emotional connotation and help the music to rise to the heights.

The names of places and people can give emotional

intensity to a poem, even a mere recital of them. Here are the lines of "Thyrsis" in which Matthew Arnold gives a list of the places he loved near Oxford:

> Runs it not here, the track by Childsworth Farm,
> Past the high wood, to where the elm-tree crowns
> The hill behind whose ridge the sunset flames?
> The signal-elm, that looks on Ilsley Downs,
> The Vale, the three lone weirs, the youthful Thames?

The emotional value is enhanced, as if by music, by the singing quality of such words as "the three lone weirs."

[5]

What are the social foundations of music?

WE MUST not suppose that composers invent their music out of the blue, without forerunners or surroundings. The innovators are the small men who set the ball rolling. The big men come at the end of a period and sum it up. Thus it was with Bach. The period of Haydn and Mozart, not to speak of the smaller people like Cherubini and Hummel, led the way to the supreme master, Beethoven. We can trace the art of Wagner through the early *Singspiele* of Adam Hiller and his contemporaries in the eighteenth century, through Weber and Marschner, to find its culmination in *Die Meistersinger* and *Tristan*. These were the right men coming at the right time and under the right circumstances; that is what enabled them to be great. Sometimes the potentially right man comes at the wrong time. Purcell, for example, was a bit too early for his flower to bloom fully; Sullivan, who in other circumstances might have written a *Figaro*, was thwarted by mid-Victorian inhibitions: the public thought that great music must be portentous and solemn, an oratorio, or a sacred cantata at the least, and that comic opera was beneath notice as a work of art.

The great example of the right man, at the right time, in the right place, is John Sebastian Bach. He was not a biological sport: he came from a long line of musical ancestors. And what is more, the musical gift did not die out with him, for he had several sons who would have shone brightly in the musical firmament if they had not been partly eclipsed by their great father. John Sebastian's first musical ancestor appears to have been Veit Bach, by profession a baker and miller, who used to spend his spare time playing on his beloved zither. Veit had a son who became a *Spielmann*, or professional musician; and from that time onward the tribe of family musicians grew until nearly every town in Thuringia had a Bach as its "town piper," as the official musicians were called. They held a humble enough position; their duty was to provide music for all civic occasions as well as for weddings, banquets, and funerals. Doubtless some little thing of their own was often played on these occasions. Then came 1685: the time was ready, the place was ready, and the circumstances were ready for the man who, to my mind, is the greatest musician of all time. J. S. Bach's position was, nominally, not much more important than that of his numerous cousins and uncles. True, Leipzig is a comparatively large town, and he was dignified by the name of "cantor," but his duties included teaching, not only music, but also Latin, to the boys at the public school. He had to play the organ, either himself or by deputy, in two churches and to conduct the services. Every week he had to provide a little thing of his own for performance on Sunday. It happened that these compositions included the *St. Matthew Passion* and the B-Minor Mass.

[6]

The Folk-Song Movement

HUBERT PARRY, in his great book *The Evolution of the Art of Music*, has shown that a Beethoven symphony, for instance, is not a unique phenomenon but that its whole structure can be traced back, stage by stage, to the art of the primitive folk singer.

The early nineteenth century started a movement among composers to short-circuit all the intervening evolutionary process and cut straight back to the origin of things. These nationalist composers tried to found their style on the folk songs of their own countries. I think the movement started in Russia when Glinka began using street songs in his operas: the idea was taken up, *con amore*, by his successors, Moussorgsky and Borodin, who not only used traditional melodies in their compositions, but built up their original work on the same basis. Even Tchaikovsky and Rachmaninoff, though they were frowned on by the ultranationalists as not being true Russians, often showed the influence of Russian folk songs in their compositions.

Members of the fashionable Russian world were shocked at anything national, as we know from Tolstoi's and Turgenev's novels, and habitually talked French to each other, reserving their native Russian for peasants and droshky drivers; therefore it is not surprising that they labelled this nationalist style as "coachman's music." But the coachman's music has survived, while the sham classical style of Rubinstein has almost disappeared.

I have just used the word "classical"; antinational musical critics are in the habit of declaring that the so-called classical style is the only true path, and that the nationalist music of the Russians, of Dvořak, and of Grieg is mere affectation or cliquishness. But what is the classical style? It is nothing more or less than the Teutonic style. It so happened that for nearly a hundred years, in the eighteenth and early nineteenth centuries, the great composers, with the possible exception of Haydn, were all German or Austrian. So the Teutonic style became accepted as the classical model. But what is the Teutonic style? When people hear a German or Austrian folk song, they say, "This is just like Mozart or Beethoven in their simpler moods; it is not a folk song at all, but was probably composed by Michael Haydn or Leopold Mozart." It never occurs to these good people that Mozart, Beethoven, and Schubert came from the humbler classes and were doubtless imbued from childhood with the popular music of their country. The truth, I believe, is not that Teutonic folk songs are like the melodies of classical composers but that the simpler melodies of classical composers are like Teutonic folk songs, and that we can claim Mozart and Beethoven as nationalists as much as Dvořak and Grieg.

Music, like language, derives ultimately from its basic beginnings. May I give an instance from my own country? About fifty years ago Cecil Sharp made his epoch-making discovery of English folk song. We young musicians were intoxicated by these tunes. We said to ourselves, "Here are beautiful melodies of which, until lately, we knew nothing. We must emulate Grieg and Smetana, and build up, on the basis of these tunes, a corpus of compositions arising out of our own country and character." And we proceeded to pour out Overtures and Rhapsodies and Ballad Operas to show the world that we were no longer a land without music. We had our critics, who took the curious line that, though it was perfectly right and proper for a Russian or a Norwegian to build up his style on his own national melodies, if an Englishman tried to do so, he was being what they described by that appalling, invented word "folky."

Of course the movement has had its camp followers: composers have thought that if they pitchforked one or two of Sharp's discoveries into a ready-made mixture imported from Russia or France they were inventing a national style. This was the bad side of the movement, and none of the more level headed of us imagined that because Beethoven quoted a Russian tune in one of his

Razumovsky quartets he thereby became a Russian composer; or that because Delius used an English folk song in one of his compositions it made him into an Englishman. Those who claim England as the birthplace of Delius' art must base their argument on more valid premises than this. The movement is now fifty years old, the tunes are again common property, and every English child must know them as well as he knows his own language, whether he likes it or not. Composers of the younger generation emphatically do not like it, but they cannot help being influenced by these beautiful tunes. As Gilbert Murray says, "The original genius is at once the child of tradition and a rebel against it."

EPILOGUE

Making Your Own Music

ALL vital art is creative art; and musical appreciation especially demands active participation rather than passive acceptance on the part of the hearer. When we listen to a symphony as we should do, we are actually taking part, with the composer and the performers, in the creation of that symphony.

Shakespeare wrote some very beautiful lines about letting music creep in our ears, but this is not a true picture of real, creative listening, which cannot exist except as a counterpart of active participation by the hearer. Therefore, before we truly listen we must be able also to create.

When I write about the creation of music, I do not mean merely putting black dots on a piece of paper. The humblest member of a choral society, the shy beginner who takes his place at the back desk of the second violins in an amateur orchestra, the child who plays a triangle in a percussion band, if he sings or plays with understanding and purpose, is a creator.

I have great admiration for the wonderful revolution in the status of music achieved in our time by the radio and the phonograph. These inventions have given to millions the opportunity to hear great music greatly played or sung. They have also set a standard for many amateurs and students of what to imitate, and occasionally, it must be confessed, of what to avoid—if they will only profit by it.

But will they so profit? Will not all this listening to superb, expert performances bring on a counsel of despair in the mind of the humble amateur, who, for example, plays the flute a little for his own amusement? Will he not feel inclined to say, "With my limited capacities, my small opportunities for practice, I cannot hope to approach the perfection which I hear. Better give up the struggle and become a merely passive listener." If our amateur flautist thinks thus, he will have lost one of the greatest assets of his spiritual life, the vision of the ultimate realities through the making of music.

Gustav Holst used to say that if a thing was worth doing at all, it was worth doing badly. I entirely agree, with this proviso—that this "doing" must be a sincere attempt toward self-expression. Superficiality, halfheartedness, sham, and swagger must have no part in the scheme. Granted this sincerity of purpose, we may well say with Calverley:

> Play, play your sonatas in A
> Heedless of what your next neighbour may say!

Music is, first and foremost, self-expression; without that it is a falsehood. I feel sure that a man marooned for life on a desert island would continue to make music for his own spiritual exaltation even though there were no one to hear him. Sometimes these spiritual exercises spread beyond the individual; the neighbours may, after all, like the results. And so we go on till we come to the famous expert whose music is for all the world. But first he must to his own self be true; he cannot then be false to any man. Wordsworth's Solitary Reaper sang for herself alone, little thinking that she was being indirectly responsible for one of the world's greatest poems.

Supposing we all became passive listeners? Whom should we find to listen to? For a time the great virtuosi who are still with us will satisfy our needs. But voices fail, fingers become stiff, vision grows dim, even in the greatest of us. Our beloved art will die of inanition unless there are young men and women to seize the torch from the faltering hands of their elders. Where are these young men and women to be found? Surely among those who are attempting to make music for themselves. How are we to discover among these the private soldier who bears the marshal's baton in his knapsack? Only by trial and error.

Music must be offered to all, though it will not be accepted by all. We must speak the password to everybody; only in that way can we find out who will respond. The many must be called so that the few may be chosen. Virginia Woolf has written: "Masterpieces are not single and solitary births, they are the outcome of many years of thinking in common, of thinking by the body of the people, so that the experience of the mass is behind the single voice."

I am not trying to exalt the dilettante at the expense of the expert. The virtuoso is essential to our musical life. The world-famous musician is like a pinnacle, shining for all to see; but unless the pinnacle rests on a solid foundation, it will totter and fall. The musical life of a community may be compared to a pyramid. At the apex are the great and famous; below, in rank after rank, stand the general practitioners of our art, competent and enthusiastic, and often endowed with a musical insight which their more famous but more specialised fellows do not possess. Here are the hard-working and unassuming men and women who are the musical salt of the earth. They wish for neither fame nor fortune; their one desire is to spread the gospel of music by precept and practice; but, like Chaucer's Poor Parson who preached the gospel of goodness, first they follow it themselves. Lastly we come to the great army of humble music makers, who, as Hubert Parry says, "make what they like and like what they make." These are the foundations of the pyramid, sustaining those above them and at the same time depending upon them for strength and inspiration. So, by laying stone on stone, we build up a great structure of music, reaching higher and higher into the empyrean but with its foundations firmly set on the great traditions of our art. Thus the humblest and the highest join in the service of music.

There is another side to this question of self-made music; as the Preacher discovered years ago, it is the business of some men to find out musical tunes. Surely if anyone ever made his own music, it was these men. But some people who ought to know better think otherwise. A foolish fellow once labelled music as the universal language. Whistler was equally foolish when he said that it was as wrong to talk about national art as national chemistry. As a climax we have Rossini's epigram, "I know only two kinds of music, good and bad."

Music, it is true, has a universal vocabulary, but each composer uses this vocabulary as his own nature and the circumstances of his surroundings dictate. We may say to Whistler that chemistry is a science whose business it is to discover and co-ordinate facts; art is the means by which one man communicates spiritually with another. As for Rossini, let me quote an example. Verdi's *Requiem* is a work which defies all the canons of good taste. It is melodramatic, sentimental, sometimes almost cheap; it employs without shame such well-worn means to excitement as the diminished seventh and the chromatic scale. Yet it is one of the greatest works of art and gained the reluctant admiration of a composer with a much different artistic philosophy, Brahms. Now, Mr. Rossini, is this good music or bad?

All young composers long to be individual and are inclined to defy the tradition in which they were brought up. This is very right and proper, but when they plunge into unknown waters, let them hold fast to the life-line of their own national tradition; otherwise the siren voices from foreign shores will lure them to destruction. Musical invention has been described as an individual flowering on a common stem. Now, young composers, do not try to be original; originality will come of itself if it is there. However individual your flowering may be, unless it is firmly grafted on the common stem, it will wither and die. I have all honour for those adventurous spirits who explore unknown regions; I cannot always follow them, but I admire their courage. Sometimes, however, I ask myself whether those composers have not even more courage who find new and unheard-of beauties along the beaten track. Try the beaten track first; if an irresistible impulse leads you into the jungle, be sure that you know the way back.

You in America have a fine literary and scholastic tradition; why not add to this a musical tradition? It is to be found in unexpected corners in this country. Do not rest until you have found it, and when it is found, do not deny your birthright. Remember what Walt Whitman said to the American poets of his time:

Come Muse migrate from Greece and Ionia,
Cross out please those immensely overpaid accounts,
That matter of Troy and Achilles' wrath, and Æneas', Odysseus' wanderings.
Placard "Removed" and "To Let" on the rocks of your snowy Parnassus,

Repeat at Jerusalem, place the notice high on Jaffa's gate and on Mount Moriah,
The same on the walls of your German, French and Spanish castles, and Italian collections,
For know a better, fresher, busier sphere, a wide, untried domain awaits, demands you.

American architects could find no classical models for their dams, grain elevators, and oil refineries; the need created the means, and now it is these buildings which are the glory of American architecture. Whitman, Lowell, and Longfellow found their best inspiration, not in classical models, but in American life and American traditions. How about American music? Until lately that was dominated by foreign influences, but a change has come over the scene. It is not for me to suggest in detail how that has come about. John Powell has experimented with a folk-song symphony; others have tried jazz. We must not make the mistake of thinking lightly of the very characteristic art of Gershwin or, to go further back, the beautiful melodies of Stephen Foster. Great things grow out of small beginnings. The American composers who wrote symphonic poems, for which they were not emotionally ready, are forgotten, while the work of those who attempted less but achieved more has become the foundation on which a great art can rise.

As a suitable ending let me quote a passage from G. M. Trevelyan's *History of England:*

One outcome of the Norman Conquest was the making of

the English language. As a result of Hastings, the Anglo-Saxon tongue, the speech of Alfred and Bede, was exiled from hall and bower, from court and cloister, and was despised as a peasants' jargon, the talk of ignorant serfs. It ceased almost, though not quite, to be a written language. The learned and the pedantic lost all interest in its forms, for the clergy talked Latin and the gentry talked French. Now when a language is seldom written and is not an object of interest to scholars, it quickly adapts itself in the mouths of plain people to the needs and uses of life. This may be either good or evil, according to circumstances. If the grammar is clumsy and ungraceful, it can be altered much more easily when there are no grammarians to protest. And so it fell out in England. During the three centuries when our native language was a peasants' dialect, it lost its clumsy inflections and elaborate genders, and acquired the grace, suppleness and adaptability which are among its chief merits. At the same time it was enriched by many French words and ideas.
. . . Thus improved, our native tongue re-entered polite and learned society as the English of Chaucer's Tales and Wycliffe's Bible, to be still further enriched into the English of Shakespeare and of Milton. There is no more romantic episode in the history of man than this underground growth and unconscious self-preparation of the despised island *patois*, destined ere long to 'burst forth into sudden blaze,' to be spoken in every quarter of the globe, and to produce a literature with which only that of ancient Hellas is comparable.[5]

Could not this fable be told also of our music in America and England? I will not weary you with Eng-

[5] London: Longmans, Green and Co., 1926, pp. 131–132. By permission.

lish sins against light, but Americans have not been blameless. What did you know of the music germinating in underground growth while the so-called educated classes, if they considered music at all, thought of it in terms of Wagner and the world's worst Festival March and of highly paid European performers showing off their fine feathers, while the real foundations of your art were neglected, with the result that for years American music consisted of watered-down imitations of European models? Even that American of all Americans, Walt Whitman, seemed to think that music consisted of nothing but Italian coloratura singers and cornets playing Verdi.

I think that both our countries are now returning to the true path. I do not wish to advocate a back-to-folksong policy. Chaucer, Shakespeare, and Milton enriched our language with cullings from France and Italy, Rome and Greece. Our music can also be enriched from foreign models, but it must be an enrichment of our native impulse and not a swamping of it. We have been too apt to think that though we could beat the foreigner at business and sport, the foreigner must necessarily beat us in questions of art. We thought that if we imitated his tricks of diction, we should achieve his inspiration, forgetting that these are only an outward and visible sign of an inward and spiritual grace, rooted in an age-old tradition.